MOTIVATIONAL & LEA
ENTREP(

So, You Want to be a Boss with Broke Pockets?

Jada Atkins © 2017

Jada Atkins © 2017

Copyright © 2017 by Jada Atkins

All rights reserved. No part of this publication may be reproduced, distributed, or transmitted in any form or by any means, including photocopying, recording, or other electronic or mechanical methods, without the prior written permission of the publisher, except in the case of brief quotations embodied in critical reviews and certain other noncommercial uses permitted by copyright law. For permission requests, write to the publisher, addressed "Attention: Permissions Coordinator," at the address below.

Jada Atkins
2479 Country Club Rd 1000B
Spartanburg, SC 29302
4jadaatkins@gmail.com

Ordering Information:
Quantity sales. Special discounts are available on quantity purchases by corporations, associations, and others. For details, contact the publisher at the address above. Orders by U.S. trade bookstores and wholesalers. Please contact Jada Atkins: Tel: (864) 561-6501 or order online at Amazon.com.

Printed in the United States of America

CONTENTS

Introduction…………………………………………………………………………………………pg. 5

Stepping out on faith as a broke entrepreneur……………………………………….pg. 6

Chapter 2

The brainstorming process of an unconventional entrepreneur…………………… pg. 9

Chapter 3

Time to show and prove what a Boss with Broke Pockets can do…………………… pg. 12

Chapter 4

Working with the tools available on a shoe string budget……………………………pg. .29

Last thoughts of a Boss with Broke Pockets……………………………………………….pg. 32

Learning Toolkit……………………………………………………………………………………. pg. 35

INTRODUCTION

Have you ever wanted to go into business for yourself, join a partnership, or co-op? Have you ever dreamed of one day employing others, or just sick and tired of working for someone's company when you could work as hard for yourself? If your answer is yes, then you are just like many of us who felt the same way. We've all considered at one point of time leaving our current employment, and starting our own business; then, reality sets in. Reality tells us that we are broke, and it would almost be impossible to come up with the startup capital needed to get a business up and running. If this sounds like you, let me be the first of many to welcome you to the "Boss with Broke Pockets Club".

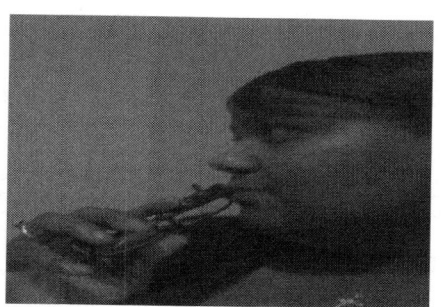

There are many books written on the market about "How to Do" or "Step by Step" to becoming a business owner. Those books are very informative but rarely do you find books addressing the issue of being broke and wanting to start your own business. Believe me when I tell you, I read lots of books, blogs, etc. but I never could find that book that would relate to me. The madness for writing and using this approach has a dual purpose. First, I want to motivate others in areas such as business and home ownership. The second part of this writing is to create an opportunity for learning, and developing appropriate writing and grammatical skills using this material as the teaching tool. At the end of this booklet, you will find suggestions for applying the tools needed to address the learning experience in becoming an efficient "broke pocket" entrepreneur.

Jada Atkins © 2017

CHAPTER 1: STEPPING OUT ON FAITH AS A BROKE ENTREPRENEUR

I was a married mother of four who lived paycheck to paycheck. We had no savings and seemed to be always struggling financially. I mainly was the bread winner and found stable employment through the manufacturing sector where I worked for over 10 years. My husband was diagnosed with having a debilitating disability, and was unable to work outside of the home. The burden to provide for the family fell on my shoulders and I could not see quitting as an option. At that time, I had 4 teenage children, a disabled husband, food and shelter to provide for my family. My health also began to fail while working in warehouses standing for 12 hours a day which became challenging to say the least. Although many things in my life seemed to be failing, I still had the determination to provide and succeed in anything I chose to do. My dreams were always to be my own boss but I never had the money or experience to go forward. I prayed and prayed and I prayed some more. I followed my heart and went into business for myself with nothing but my last paycheck. Every step forward was on the faith of a mustard seed and all the money I had in the world which was only five hundred dollars. Only God and I knew how much I really needed my business venture to succeed.

.

By sharing my entrepreneurial experience through a series of short stories, I hope that you will learn what not to do in a startup business, give motivation to my fellow Bosses with Broke Pockets and finally yet uniquely allow English Professionals to use this book as a teaching tool in grammatical writing and errors. I wrote this book in an unconventional and creative way because I am a uniquely unconventional entrepreneur. I have learned to embrace my uniqueness.

After I made the tough and scary decision to transition from being the employee to employer, I felt a since of pride growing within me. Pride was one feeling but I had many more to go along with that. The feeling of urgency overwhelmed me and a lack of confidence in myself were the worst feeling ever. But how could I step out on faith, yet feel this awful? Did I truly understand the faith I was stepping out on? Was It God I was hearing or was that my own selfish desires that manifested? Where will the funding come from? Wow! Those were real thoughts and it made me question what I was doing and if I made a major mistake. Now I know that was just normal jitters for a broke entrepreneur(chuckles).

In the beginning, I had no clue on what kind of service or product I would provide. I had no business plan and very little money but I did have a free office space for 3 months in a prime location, a pending lawsuit that could possibly help me to fund my business, plenty of prayers and the determination to succeed. I always felt my purpose was to help others and I had just as much desire to do so.

The first job in my life was as a babysitter and cutting neighbor's grass. By age 12 I was as a candy striper at Maryland General Hospital; that was one of the most rewarding jobs I ever held and yet it didn't come with a paycheck, just free lunch and bus tokens. At 21, I found myself feeling the need to volunteer again. I ended up volunteering through AmeriCorps, the Magic Me Program; another life changing and rewarding experience for me. Again, I always knew in my heart my calling was to help people. I have a rule of thumb that I live by, any good thing that keep reoccurring in your dreams can manifest in your life; God may be giving you your blue print or business plan through your dreams.

Sassy.Org
Sharing A Sister Social Youth Organization

Share A Sister Social Organization was a group I founded started in 2014. It was formed as a mentoring program and as a creative space for females with an entrepreneurial spirit. Members came from various backgrounds and much to offer. Our oldest member was over 70 years young. Eventually, it was dissolved due to low participation.

CHAPTER 2: The Brainstorming Process of an Unconventional Entrepreneur

I believe when you take on a project, you must be realistic in every aspect of the project. If you are not careful, you can find yourself over budget before you get started good. If you are like me and many other aspiring entrepreneurs on the low end of the financial pool, then you may not have proper funding to start your own business. I'm certain that it would be much easier if you knew where your funding was coming from. This is the most unconventional way of starting off a business venture, again there is nothing conventional about me nor would I suggest that you start off your journey this way. My way is by far the hardest way to start off.

I am not an attorney, but I do suggest you seek funding before attempting to start your own business. Do your research and seek professional help when taking on such a project.

I found out early on in my journey of being a boss with broke pockets, I had to become creative. I had to figure out how to achieve basic goals without money in my pocket. For example, In the beginning, I had to figure out how to secure essential business accounts without any money. It threw me for a loop since I had never opened a business or corporate account before. Every time I dial a number inquiring about setting up a business account, I think I held my breath every time the representative began to speak. Little did I know, I did not need money when setting up an account, all was needed was the proper information for the business.

Wasn't that a relief? Now I had given myself permission to breathe again. Although I had all my proper paper work etc. that showed proof of my legitimacy, somehow, I did not feel like one. Maybe it was the lack of confidence I had in my ability to succeed. That was my first time acknowledging that I was a boss with broke pockets and giving up was not an option. My whole life was depending on my success; it felt as if I was fighting for the life of me and my family.

Jada Atkins © 2017

Note: Over thinking a situation could be the worst self-inflicted torture you could ever put yourself through. Do your homework, research everything, and ask the question. There are no dumb questions.

For an unconventional person, brainstorming could be a bit overwhelming, a bit sobering and a lot of creative thinking. Because I've never been one to ask for assistance, I found it to be very challenging for me. I became anxiously overwhelmed at the thought of asking anyone for money. Not only do I have no experience at asking for money but how do I ask someone to loan or invest in my new company? By investing in my new startup company, that would mean they would be ultimately investing in me.

With no experience, how would I approach them? What is the proper way to ask for a loan? If I asked them to invest, what should I offer them as a return on their investments? If my family and friends say no, how will that affect our relationship? Will they laugh at me? These were some of the questions I asked myself every time the thought came to my mind to ask for help getting started. I decided that I was not prepared to hear the no answer from my loved ones, so I never asked. I did decide to run the idea pass my mother who have always been my biggest supporter and fan; her opinion means a lot to me.

After talking with my mom, my mom suggested that she withdraw from her 401k account and gift me with a few thousand dollars to help me on my journey a boss with broke pockets. Boy oh boy, I was so over joyed that I could jump out of my skin! I was happy that I did not have to ask for help, eventually I would have asked my mom for help (chuckles). Who know their children better than a mother? No one. I am convinced that my mom knew it was difficult for me to ask, so she offered. My mom just wanted to see me go after my dreams and be a part of the manifestation of my dreams. I am forever grateful. Once again, I told myself that failure is not an option and it was to many people depending on me to succeed. I stepped out on the faith of a mustard seed because I knew it was God's plan! Little did my mom know, she gave me a little bit more confidence.

Jada Atkins © 2017

You are probably still wondering, what is so unconventional about my journey? Conventual people would never attempt a project of this magnitude on a less than shaky foundation and without having it all planned. So, why did I? Because I am not conventual, nor was I ever offered free office rental space to explore the idea of being self-employed. For you to fully understand, I must explain a bit further.

In October of 2013, I had an on the job injury that fractured my ankle bone. Little did I know, that fractured ankle would expose me to a bone disease that I had not known about previously. After walking around on a painful fractured ankle for 3 months, my doctor told me that I would never be able to do the type of work I was accustomed to for over 10 years. Although it was devastating news, I knew I would still have to be able to provide for my family. But I had not yet considered becoming self-employed; not until February 2014.

During this time, I was searching for a bigger home rental space and a coworker referred me to her landlord office manager. After several long conversations with the manager, the manager and I developed a great repour. After mentioning my natural sales and customer service skills, she offered me an office rental space for 3 months free with water and electric included. I turned down the offer 2 separate times. Then the fear of total unemployment set in; that was a scary feeling. I decided that one opportunity was better than none and I always knew that I was destined to become a business owner. With $500, no business plan and no idea of the service I would offer, I accepted her offer the third time around. When she placed those keys in my hand; somehow, I felt empowered and I knew for certain that failure was not an option for me. *Recap: A mother and wife of 4, living paycheck to paycheck, with a disable husband and now I was diagnosed with a debilitating disease, no business plan and now a legitimate business with a set of office keys and the faith of a mustard seed. Yes, I agree it's a lot to take in.*

Jada Atkins © 2017

CHAPTER 3: TIME TO SHOW AND PROVE WHAT A BROKE POCKET BOSS CAN DO

When I first stepped into my first very own office, it felt amazing and for the first time I could remember feeling proud of myself. Although intimidating, I had a job to do and I intended on getting it done. After bringing my personal computers, a couple desk and chairs purchased from good will, a few supplies, and a welcoming smile to the office, I was ready to start my new career. Now it was time for me to decide the service I would provide.

After exploring my community needs intensively, I found that many families were living below poverty and some had never stepped foot out of their community. I wanted to be the person to bring hope back into the lives of some community residents. Leisure travel popped in my head and that is where my business started from. That was one creative year and it built up a little more confidence in my ability to succeed.

Over the last 3 years, my company and I have evolved into something I am so proud of. With over 100 clients and 85% of them returning, I am happy to say that my service has made a difference in the lives of over 100 clients. I have found my niche and I ran with it. The opportunity I creatively created for myself have presented many opportunities for growth.

Did I mention that I am the only full-time employee and wear all hats? Everything I learned over that last 3 years have been self-taught. There have been many crash courses during the 3 years, good thing I am a quick learner.

Note: It is said that most new startup business fail within the first 3 years.

When I made the 3 years mark, I had to pinch myself because this broke pocket boss was still thriving. How surprise was I when I realized that I did not owe anyone a single penny, I learned and executed my own marketing, I learned to effectively network and present my service professionally, I learned to take notes and pay close attention. Since then, I have been offered roles on boards and committees. It has truly been a life changing event.

TIME TO SHOW AND PROVE

The logo's, advertisements and picture are a glimpse of current and pass products and services.

Jada Atkins © 2017

SASSY.ORG
SHARE A SISTER SOCIAL YOUTH ORGANIZATION

SASSY.ORG
Share A Sister Social Youth Organization

JF& Company
WORLDWIDE

Jada Atkins © 2017

JF & Company

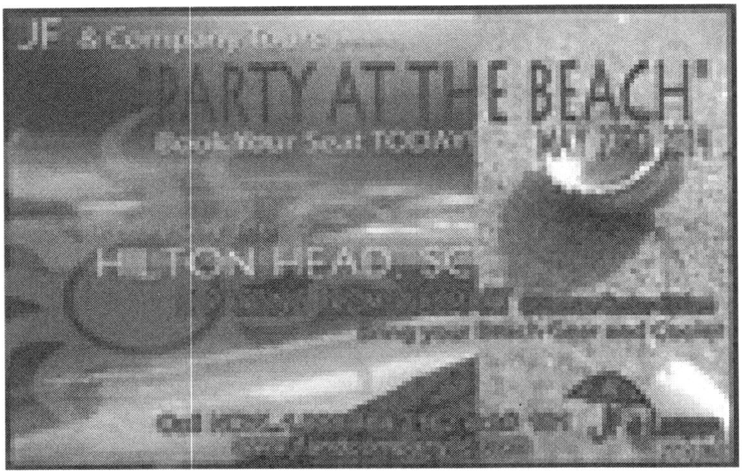

Jada Atkins © 2017

Sassy.Org

Share A Sister Social Youth Organization

864.327.9086 www.sassyorg.com

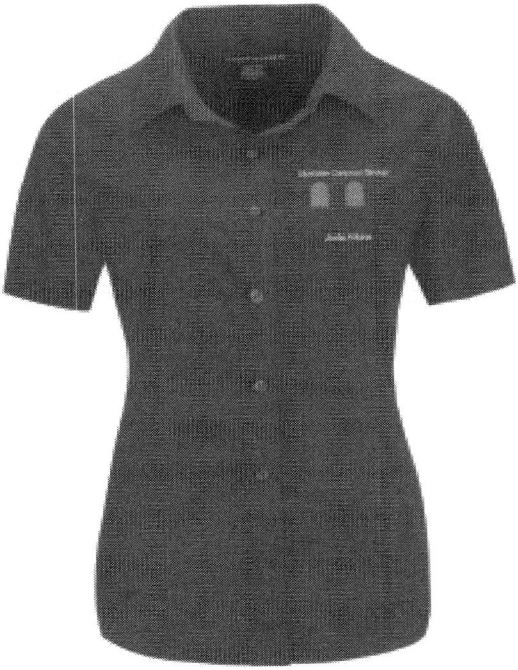

Jada Atkins © 2017

Need a Ride?   JF & Company, LLC Transportation Services

Safe, Reliable, Dependable
Reasonable Rates-Individuals, Groups, Long-term Needs
One-way or Round Trips - No Distance Too Short

Phone: (864) 327-9121 or 327-9066 or 1-888-484-2182 ext. 101

Car broken down? No License? Group too Big? Don't want to ask family or friends?

We will get you to work, doctor/dental visits, the airport, court, grocery store, pharmacy, to visit an incarcerated loved one. Where do you need to go? Churches, Assisted Living Facilities, Schools, and extra room without taking an extra bus? - let us fill the gap.

Don't let lack of transportation limit your life!

103 East Kennedy Street, Spartanburg, SC 29306
jada@jfandcompanyllc.com
Office Hours: Mon-Sat 9:30-5:30

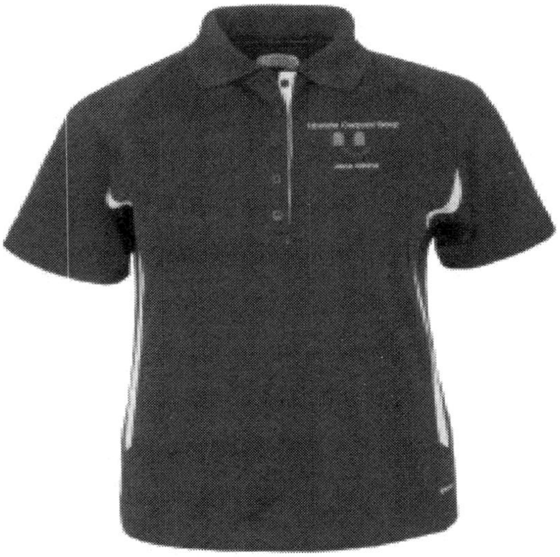

Jada Atkins © 2017

.A luncheon event I attended my first few months in business. It is important to invest in events that could bring your business recognition, to stay relevant, and a great opportunity to network

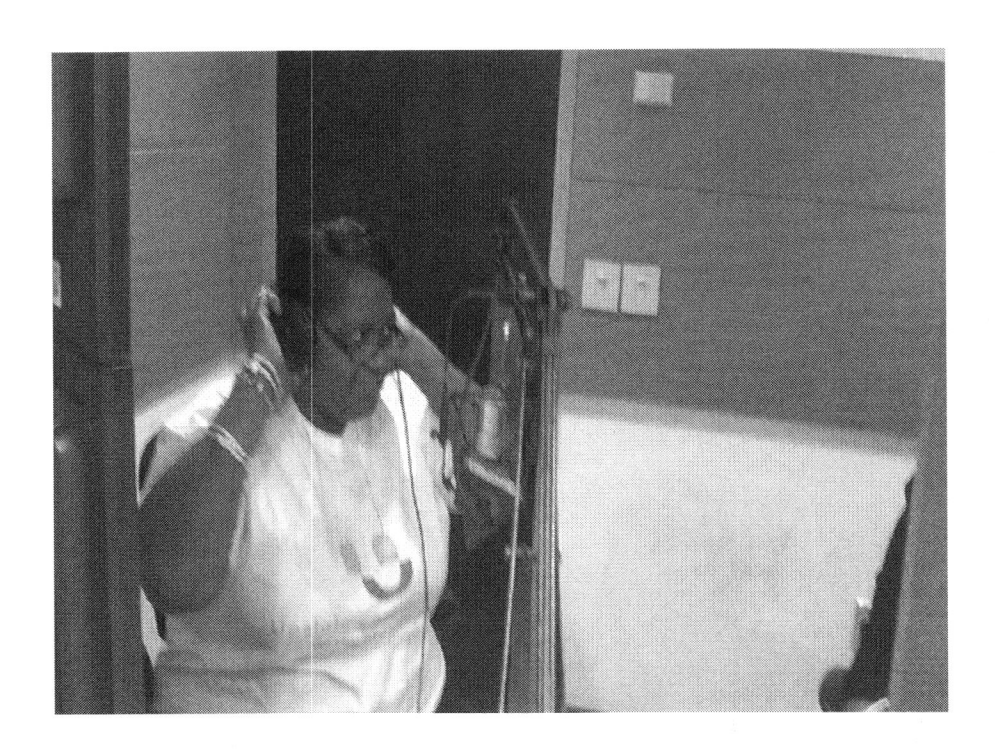

This was a very proud day for me as a Boss with Broke Pockets. I was doing an interview promoting a 501(c) (3) nonprofit organization I founded. Truly one of the highlights of my early career.

Jada Atkins © 2017

Jada Atkins © 2017

FIND LIFE COALITION

Jada Atkins © 2017

Be Sweat 2 Retreat

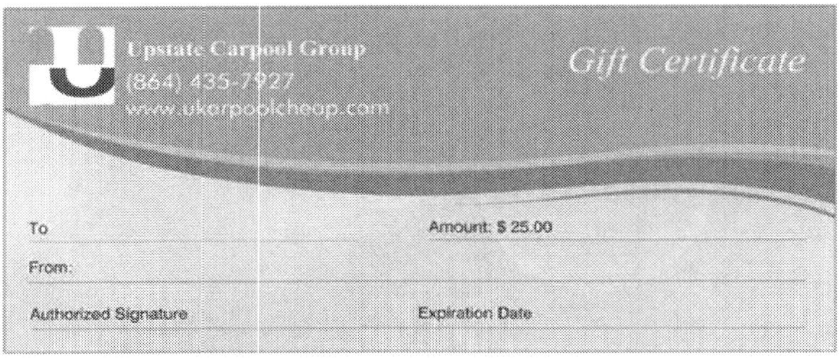

Jada Atkins © 2017

CHAPTER 4: WORKING WITH THE TOOLS AVAILIBLE ON A SHOE STRING BUDGET

In this section, I will talk and touch bases on how to execute your to do list on a shoe string budget. I can't state it enough time, I am not an attorney and you should seek professional help when making decisions about your business. Ultimately you are responsible for your business.

Creativity came into play when trying to execute certain project with little money and no experience to speak of. My approach was to tackle things head on research, budget, and implement. Many business owners can hire people to do the research, create the budget and implement the plans. But for a broke pocket boss, it may not be a feasible option. Your only other option is to wear whatever hat needed to accomplish your project goal. This includes the hat of learning how to write effectively, and presenting professionally prepared presentations.

In the beginning, I had to determined how I wanted to structure my business. Would I structure it as corporation, limited liability, partnership, or sole proprietorship? Research the internet for information on business structures and requirement. Seek dialog with other business owners who is willing to lend direction and a listening ear. It would be a good idea to ask other business owner for referrals; you may be surprised at the savings a referral can bring. Ask for lead referrals from other business owners, but don't be overly disappointed if other business owners aren't receptive to your need. Become knowledgeable about events free or at minimum cost to you. Your local library may have rental space available for your usage at a low cost.

Every startup business will need some equipment and it could be a budget crusher if you are not careful of your spending. Before you decide to go for broke consider this tip, search your local Goodwill and Salvation Army for slightly used equipment. I saved hundreds shopping there and could find everything I needed for my offices. Think of it like this, would you go to Longhorn Steak House with McDonald money in your pocket? I know I wouldn't show up at a place like that with $5 in my pocket. I agree that I maybe a boss with broke pockets but by no means am I delusional.

Marketing strategies and budgets are just as important; in my opinion, marketing is one of the most important parts of a good business plan. It can also prove to be a budget crusher if you are not careful. Here are a few tips that will help you along. When thinking of cost effective ways of advertising and marketing, think of social media. Remember this, if you are already on social media, then you already have access to thousands of potential client or customers. I would start there by performing my own surveys, introducing my product to my social media friends and feel out potential clients or customers. Most times you will get honest opinions from your friends on social media. Don't be afraid of honest opinions. Honest opinions will help you to refine your product and or service. I made my share of mistakes in this area my first year in business. Social media is just as good as word of mouth. Word of mouth has also proven to be the most effective means of advertising and the absolute cheapest; nothing is cheaper than free.

Another effective way of advertising your service or product is to network. It is important to introduce and affiliate your business with other business owners and community leaders. If you get an invite to participate in a job fair, work shop or community meeting, plan on attending as many as possible. This will prove to be a great way of getting your brand out and gain useful information. You will need to put on a stunning performance every time you participate in these type events.

Brochures are also a great advertisement tool. With the average computer, you can create beautiful brochures on your own. Brochures show basic information and service or products your company provides. Brochures can also be left in public locations, mailed to potential client's or customers and used as flyers. It all can be done in house and you will save by cutting out the middle man. If you are not comfortable with designing your own brochure, consult a professional.

In my closing, I just want to touch basis about startup capital for the new business venture. *Again, I must state, I am not an attorney or a professional on any of these subjects. Based on my own unconventional strategies and mistakes made in the early stages of my journey to becoming a boss with broke pockets, I would never suggest my method to anyone.*

I would like to urge all aspiring entrepreneurs to do your research, do the homework before taking on such a huge and life changing challenge; you will appreciate it later. There are many options to funding your dreams. First try asking your friends and family. If you don't have any luck, try a personal loan. Maybe that was a strike out as well. Then try researching websites like SBA to find out if you qualify for funding through different programs. Use your saving to fund your dreams; if you are not willing to take a chance on you, then who will? Take on a second job for a while and save what you can to fund your dream. The best part about funding yourself, you won't owe anyone for funding you.

I believe you can achieve anything you put your mind too. Although I would not recommend anyone to start a business the way I did, I do recommend you chase your dreams and put more than 100% of your efforts into it. If you intend on not making it to the finish line, don't waste your time or money. For those bosses with broke pockets who intend on finishing strong, I will meet you at the finish line. Good luck on your journey my friends.

With Love,

Jada Atkins

Last Thoughts of a Boss with Broke Pockets

This have been one rollercoaster of a ride, a very lonely ride might I add. I found out through my entrepreneurial journey, envy will rear its ugly head. Friends and family will smile at you, verbally claim to support you; yet will not give you free thumbs up or down on social media to support you or your venture. Solid relationships will become nonexistent when you begin to strive to reach your dream. I'm not convinced it is jealousy, I think people can't stand to see you chase your dream only because they are afraid to chase their own. It will take thick skin to emotionally get through that process; once you are over it, it become a thing of the pass. When I experienced the feeling of loneliness during a time when I should have been at my happiest point, I started to detach my personal feelings and focus on birthing a beautiful business. I want you to know that God supplies all our needs. Strangers will come out of nowhere and help you bring your vision full circle. Believe in you and your product, stand by your word, never accept failure as an option, do the work, do the research and wear every hat you need to succeed on your journey. Remember you did not go into business to impress others or for others approval, you went on this journey for you and your future. Don't give people that kind of power over you. Push hard, push pass and push through the obstacles that will come your way. I believe in your ability to succeed

Jada Atkins

I DREAMED BIG AS A LITTLE GIRL

GIVING UP IS NERVER AN OPTION!

So, You Want to Be a Boss with Broke Pockets? Learning Toolkit

One of my most challenging basic problems in organizing, and developing the business document were the writing and complying the information grammatically correct. No, I am not a shame to say it since shame plays "no part" in ownership. Therefore, the body of this book has been intentionally left in this format. It is designed this way to help you define, and improve upon your basic sentence structure and writing skills. The body of this booklet is recommended to be used as a tangible tool for discovering, correcting, and creating sample formats to followed as you pursue your dreams.

Hints:

- Can you find, and correct the grammatical errors?
- What are the standards used to satisfy a proper paragraph?
- Punctuations if not properly used, will distort and make it difficult for the reader to understanding your intent.

TOOLKIT NOTES

TOOLKIT NOTES

TOOLKIT NOTES

TOOLKIT NOTES

TOOLKIT NOTES

TOOLKIT NOTES

TOOLKIT NOTES

TOOLKIT NOTES

Made in the USA
Columbia, SC
19 January 2022